D0623214

Thanks Mom for letting God continually use you as the 'Backbone' to our family.
Bonnie L. Johnson Greene, your sacrificial labor of love will be rewarded.
For God is not unrighteous to forget your work and labor of love....Hebrews 6:10
--CC
(Holy Bible. KJV., © 2003 by Thomas Nelson, Nashville, Tennessee 37214, USA)

Published in the United States by
In Writing Publications L.L.C
nwritingpublications@gmail.com

ISBN: 978-0-578-87385-5 (Hardcover) E-Book available via publisher
Copyright © June 2020

Library of Congress Control Number: 2020912835

Photograph Credits
Photographs courtesy of Fred Gregory Family Archive

Acknowledgements
Nick Thomas, Communicator Astronaut Encounter; Kennedy
Space Center
The History Makers ® VIdeo Oral History Interview with Col.
Frederick D. Gregory, July 27, 2007. The History Makers African
American Video Oral History Collection, 1900 S. Michigan Ave,
Chicago, Illinois

No copyright infringement intended.

  Col Fred Gregory, U.S. Astronaut: A Children's Pictorial Biography

nwritingpublications@gmail.com

Layout and Illustration

www.designbybryn.com
brynzaid@gmail.com

Dad's Mission

A Pictorial Biography of Colonel Frederick Drew Gregory, U.S. Astronaut

I am a flip book! Start on this page and flip through to watch the rocket take off.

FORWARD
From Frederick Gregory

I am certain that I had the best Dad and mentor in the world. He did not know the word "No". My questions and requests of him were answered in the affirmative. Dad would seem to wait until I proved that his answers were wrong. This upbringing sparked a sense of exploration and limitless adventure in me as a child growing up amidst notable figures like General Benjamin O. Davis, Jr. and my own "Uncle Charlie" Drew, the Physician.

I was privileged to grow up during a time where there was a greater sense of "Us". We all knew that what one member did affected the other. There was a real community network that fostered an expectation of excellence. If you messed up at school, before reaching home the entire neighborhood would reprimand you----even at church on Sunday morning there would be an 'Eleventh Commandment' about what you should have done. My own Mother, as a Teacher, thought I was in the 5th grade... ALL of my life. There was an unspoken expectation that, ' you WILL be productive' , regardless of what obstacles arose. Dad would say, ["You have got to give the next generation more than what you have in your own. Constantly raise the bar. CONTRIBUTE"] .

This inherent desire to succeed at whatever task given started way before me. Perhaps my Grandfather James Francis Gregory, a graduate of Amherst and Yale, initiated the drive. Even though my forefather J. M. Gregory (a Howard University Graduate) was denied his appointment to West Point because of his race, he kept producing. That generation never sat around complaining about what they were not allowed to do. They found a way to pursue excellence.

Whether it was knowing at 14 years of age when I met my wife Barbara, I would marry her, have a family, a career, to now public speaking. I hope the legacy continues to reach as many that will accept the Challenge. Accomplish your mission.

Frederick Drew Gregory, US Astronaut

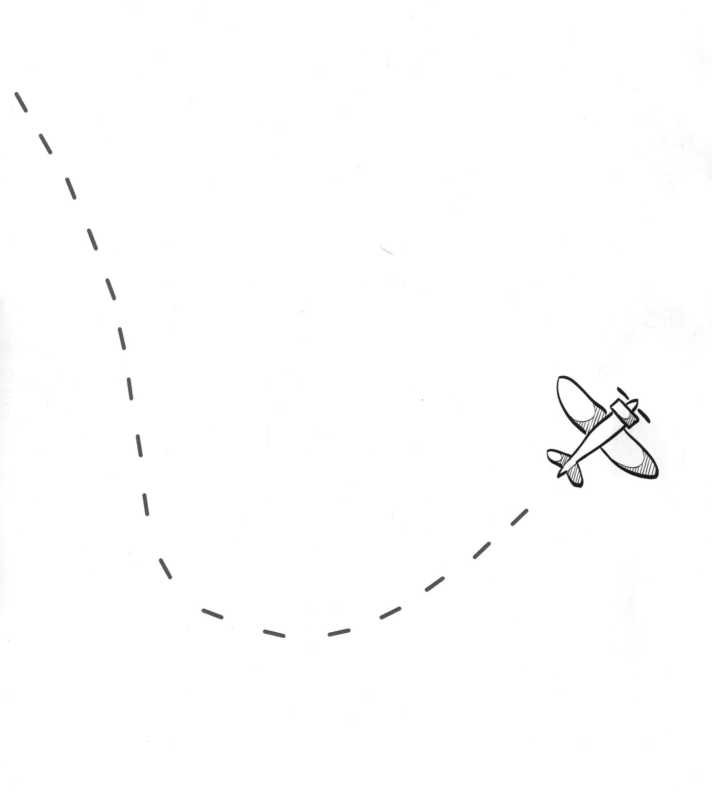

"Bam!" "Bam!" "Bam!" "Bam!" "Bam!"
That was the roaring rapping sound of my Mother vehemently banging on the window of *"Bennie's"* red- striped white Luscombe.

"You'll **NOT** take my boy up in the air."
It was then that I knew, although DAD previously said, "Sure, he can go up for a ride"; it was Mother who ruled the roost.

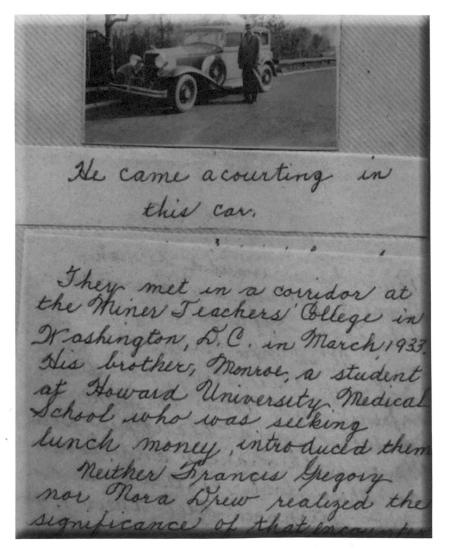

He came acourting in this car.

They met in a corridor at the Miner Teachers' College in Washington, D.C. in March 1933. His brother, Monroe, a student at Howard University Medical School who was seeking lunch money, introduced them. Neither Francis Gregory nor Nora Drew realized the significance of that encounter.

    I had to settle for a taxi around the runway while hoisted up on the 3-4 inch thick Yellow Page Telephone Directory Book. For some reason, Mother, an Elementary School Teacher from Washington, D.C., didn't think a World War II combat fighter pilot was qualified to take her 5 year old son for an airplane ride.

    Little did she know that ride would spark my mind to reach for what I thought was the most fascinating adventure of the time; a fast ride to the open skies. Dad would fuel it by taking me to countless events at Andrews AFB. Many leisurely afternoons were spent lying on a hillside watching not only airplanes, but sports car races that General Curtis LeMay authorized. To this day, I still love the sound of a Ferrari shifting gears along with the distinctly delightful smell of aviation fuel.

My husband was a Leader - Teacher - Principal of two high schools - Asst Supt of D.C. Schools. Official in Labor Department Humanitarian - Christian God's gift to all of us

ASST. SUPERINTENDENT GREGORY MOVES TO DEPARTMENT OF LABOR

Assistant Superintendent Francis A. Gregory will be assistant director of manpower development at the U.S. Department of Labor on December 1. His work will concern manpower, automation, and training.

He leaves the Washington school system after thirty years, during which he has been principal of Phelps Vocational School and later of Armstrong Technical High School, and assistant superintendent of industrial and adult education, his present position. Before appointment to Washington schools, he taught mathematics and physics at North Carolina Agricultural and Technical College and industrial electricity at Tuskegee. His degrees in electrical engineering are from the Case Institute of Technology and from MIT.

Mr. Gregory is chairman of the Superintendent's committee on human relations and is a member of DCEA's committee on ethics. He has given untiring service to the community through a great variety of organizations and activities

Asst. Superintendent
Francis A. Gregory

Top: Dad

Bottom Left: Mother

Bottom Right: Dad with Frederick

Dad had an endless supply of knowledge and energy. As an avid tennis player, he not only graduated from Case Institute in Ohio, he was accepted at MIT for the Electrical Engineering program. Unfortunately, during the 1930's EE research and application jobs were not available for ambitious "Negros". Even though he had taught at Carolina A & T and Tuskegee Institute, he had to secure a position teaching high school.

It was at that point in life that he met Miss Nora Drew, my mother. His passion ignited in me, his only child, a thirst for exploration and limitless DISCOVERY.

As a Boy Scout, at 12, my troop traveled over 2,000 miles by train from the U.S. capital to a ranch in Irvine, California. This encounter with over 50,000 Jamboree attendees unaccompanied by my parents, was preceded by 7 - 8 week summer camps as a 7 and 8 year old boy. I never once needed the post cards Mother sent requesting her to come rescue me once homesick. I STILL have those postcards.

One pivotal day while watching the F-100 Thunderbird Pilot Lt. Creech, I approached and asked how I might become one.

"Your chances would increase if you attend the new school being built in Colorado Springs, Colorado". I had been there before! My scouting days of traveling had already familiarized me with the area when we climbed Pikes Peak. Before the site was even permanently selected, I set my sights for the New Air Force Academy. Although, it was understood that I was supposed to attend Amherst like my forefathers.

Our Family.
Freddie -
Air Force
Academy

I had the opportunity to take courses in Political Science, Economics, Law, and History while majoring in Military Engineering. (The abundance of credit hours taken in Classical English today would be considered a minor). While shaking the hand of General LeMay, the Chief of Staff of the Air Force, at graduation, oblivious to the long line of cadets, we engaged in a lengthy conversation about fast cars. It was he, that Dad and I heard racing through the runway. One never knows who they might meet later in life.

Frederick Drew Gregory

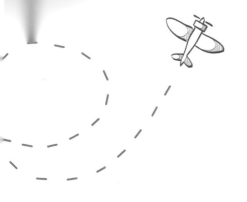

"Back in the Day" Washington, D.C. Party

Just Married

Barbara and Frederick Gregory

As the 6th graduating class of the United States Air Force Academy, I considered my classmates as the brothers I never had; great Americans, patriots, and heroes. Unlike my Dad, we were able to pursue our careers and remain lifelong friends despite our differences. With all of the academic rigor, I found time to get married on Graduation Day,

12

June 3, 1964 to the beautiful Barbara
Archer. My new bride and I were off to
Randolph AFB (San Antonio), Texas.

Despite the harassment for not going
off to fighter pilot training; Helicopters it
was! Later, while I served as a Search and
Rescue Helicopter pilot at Danang AB,
Barbara held down the fort - even traveling
alone from D. C. to Hawaii visiting me
with our toddler and newborn in tow.

After the excitement and thrill of saving folks, once back from Vietnam, I needed a new CHALLENGE. With my life goal of making a contribution, I decided it might as well be fun too! While at Whiteman AFB, Missouri, I discovered that I could apply for Test Pilot School and cross train to 'fixed winged' aircraft. So, I transitioned from flying a helicopter at 90 KTS (knots) to a fighter of 900 KTS. Why not complete both trainings at the same time?

Barbara and baby Frederick, Jr

"Ridiculous!" was the Navy skipper's
response to such a request that proved to
be successful. With my family's support,
instead of returning to South East Asia,
I headed off to Test Pilot School with
the Navy. Although this was some of
the most CHALLENGing coursework I
had to handle, it led to the qualifications
that the National Aeronautics & Space

Administration was looking for at Langley Research Center. Though I originally signed a two year contract, I ended up staying with NASA for 35 years before retiring.

Dad always told me, *"Tomorrow you should do something you thought impossible the day before"*.

When General Davis, the pilot's feet that I sat under as a 5 year old suggested I apply for the Astronaut Program, it took only one more persuasion. The original Star Trek actress Nichelle Nichols (Lt. Uhura, the communications officer on the weekly television series) was hired to encourage minorities and women to apply for the Space Shuttle program. Her persuasive speech, along with the very form-fitting blue uniform, convinced me that this was the position for me.

| | BRANDENSTEIN | BUCHLI | COATS | COVEY | CREIGHTON |

| GARDNER | GIBSON | GREGORY | GRIGGS | HART |

| HOFFMAN | LUCID | McBRIDE | McNAIR | MULLANE |

| ONIZUKA | RESNIK | RIDE | SCOBEE | SEDDON |

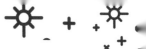

After countless hours of training, the day finally came from flying HH-43F's to commanding a Space Shuttle. Funny, with all the advances in technology, we still had to take a bus to the spacecraft. It was quite humbling to be among the first group of candidates known as Thirty-Five New Guys although there were Gals too.

During the take off so many things flashed through my mind...Barb, the kids, the crew. This time that banging against the window was the booming eruption

of the engine's ignition and not my mother's precautions.

Too late! No more 'taxi' rides. That initial take-off would turn into three... the orbiters CHALLENGER, DISCOVERY, and ATLANTIS. Although now on display as Museum pieces, Mission Accomplished!

Headed for Mars?

Historical Overview

Frederick Drew Gregory, Sr. (born January 7, 1941) is the son of Francis A. Gregory (1907-1977) and Nora Drew Gregory (1913-2011), the sister of the African American researcher and surgeon Dr. Charles Drew. He has earned degrees from George Washington University and the US Air Force Academy. As an Air Force pilot, he flew 550 combat missions over Vietnam as a rescue helicopter pilot. For this heroism, he was awarded the Distinguished Flying Cross among many other notable citations. While on the homefront, his wife Barbara (married June 3, 1964 on USAFA Graduation Day until her death in 2008) was ensuring that his legacy would continue by giving birth to his son Frederick Jr. (1964) and daughter Heather Lynn (1966).

Upon his return to the United States he attended Test Pilot School with the Navy at Patuxent Naval Air Station in Lexington Park, MD. Although incomprehensible at the time, Gregory successfully completed the rotary (helicopters) AND fixed wing course of study. This acquisition for the military and his 1978 NASA selection led to approximately 7,000 hours of flight time in 50 types of aircraft. Astronaut Gregory flew three shuttle missions: STS-51B in 1985 as a pilot; STS-33 (1989); and STS-44 (1991). He would not only be selected as the 1st African American Commander, but would serve as the 1st African American Deputy Administrator and Acting NASA Administrator. This adventurous lifestyle began well before his space travels.

As a youth he would travel cross country without his parents accompaniment on Scouting trips or attend Jack & Jill events. Following Atlantis as an escort, upon seeing for the first time the level of stress the risk taking missions had upon the families, Col. Gregory ended his space career. With what he thought would be a difficult decision, he was met with Barbara's response of, "that's nice...could you take the trash out?" Clearly life would continue. Fred, Jr., would later go on to graduate from Stanford University, while Heather, Sweet Briar College (each producing fine families of their own).

Frederick D. Gregory, now married to the former Annette Becke of Washington, D.C., has 7 grandchildren and countless mentees. He and Annette spend time public speaking, traveling, boating, and still enjoying fast cars.

Drew & Gregory Descendants:
1985 Challenger Launch

A-3

FAMILY

LEGACY

Bibliography

Boy Scouts of America ©. National Service Center: Irving, Texas

Creech, W.L. (1927-2003) WWII, Vietnam; General; Distinguished Service Command Pilot experienced in 40 different military aircraft; U.S. Aerial Demonstration Team (Thunderbirds). Official United States Air Force Website, USAF News.

Davis, Benjamin O. Jr. (1912-2002) WWII, Korean War; General; Commander 99th Fighter Squadron "Tuskegee Airmen". Distinguished Unit Citation, March 24, 1945 Smithsonian National Air and Space Museum Archives.

Drew, Charles. (1904-1950) U.S. Surgeon; Pioneered methods of storing blood plasma for transfusion; Organized one of the large-scale blood bank in the U.S. "Uncle Charlie".

Jack and Jill of America, Inc. founded 1938; Washington, D.C. Headquarters.

LeMay, Curtis. (1906-1990) WWII; General; 1947 Commander USAF in Europe; Organized Air Operations for the famous Berlin Airlift, 5th Chief of Staff USAF Distinguished Service. Official United States Air Force Website, USAF News.

Nichols, Nichelle. (1932-present). American Actress and Singer. Best Known Role "Lieutenant Uhura" Star Trek. NASA Board of Directors invited to participate in the Astronaut Recruitment Program. © 1990-2019 by IMDb.com,Inc.

Star Trek the Original Series 1969- Gene Roddenberry – Hollywood, CA United States.

Educational Exploration
(Classroom Application)

1. Research some of the additional historical figures found throughout the book.

   Political: Former United States President George Bush and First Lady Barbara Bush;

   Military: United States Air Force Generals Curtis LeMay, Benjamin O. Davis, Jr, and W.L. Creech;

   Medical: Dr. Charles Drew;

   Space: Astronauts Ron Mc Nair, Shannon Lucid;

   Entertainment: Nichelle Nichols, Star Trek;

   Organizations: National Aeronautics & Space Administration, Scouts of America, and Jack & Jill of America

2. Practice geography skills:

   a. Locate latitude and longitude coordinates of the Southeast Asia country Vietnam

   b. Calculate the distance travelled throughout various states mentioned in the book.

   c. Indicate, using a compass rose, the direction the space shuttle traveled leaving Cape Canaveral, Florida.

3. Calculate total distance traveled in a single orbit using the Earth's circumference and the altitude.

4. Research how Global Positioning Satellite (GPS) mapping correlates to space exploration

5. Visit Space Shuttle Discovery in the National Air and Space Museum (Smithsonian Institute) and Space Shuttle Atlantis at the Kennedy Space Center

6. Locate the names of the Space Shuttles mentioned in the story.

From the Author

When one of my sons was assigned the task of reporting on a historical figure who contributes to the lives of Americans, my husband responded,

"My USAFA Mentor, whom we referred to as our Air Force Dad; Col Fred Gregory of course!"

Every excerpt we found was not written with a 2nd grader in mind; much less any elementary student at all. Thus, we accepted the CHALLENGE of creating our own literary piece briefly chronicling the life of the **United States Air Force Pilot, Vietnam Veteran, Astronaut, former Deputy Administrator for NASA, Husband, Father, Grandfather, and Mentor to many world-wide.** Although the audience is intended for children [and classroom implementations for teachers], the historical data can be beneficial to all generations of readers alike.

About the Author

Charlotte Cosby is the wife of USAFA Graduate and Pilot Col (Ret). Ricky Cosby. Together they have 11 children and 6 grandchildren. Prior to traveling the globe as a United States Air Force Spouse, she taught Elementary Education in the district of Springfield (MO) Public Schools and later homeschooled their children. She holds a Bachelor of Arts, with Honors Degree and a Master of Arts in Elementary Education Degree from Drury College (now University).

Fred Gregory &
Rick Cosby, (USAFA
class of 1977)

Charlotte Cosby,
Author

Makeup: Wedding Glam Miami
Hair: Angel Hair Braids of Beverly Hills

CPSIA information can be obtained
at www.ICGtesting.com
Printed in the USA
BVHW021722050421
604206BV00005B/69